After I Stop Lying

After I Stop Lying

Poems by Deborah Bacharach

Cherry Grove Collections

Published by Cherry Grove Collections
P.O. Box 541106
Cincinnati, OH 45254-1106

ISBN: 9781625491244
LCCN: 2015931881

Poetry Editor: Kevin Walzer
Business Editor: Lori Jareo

Visit us on the web at www.cherry-grove.com

Acknowledgements

My thanks to the editors of publications in which these poems originally appeared, often in earlier versions and with different titles:

- *10x3 plus*: "Welcome to America"
- *The Antigonish Review*: "Still Life"
- *Arts and Letters*: "The Landscape," "The Last Few Days Before Christmas"
- *Blood Orange Review*: "Secrets"
- *Calyx*: "The New Joke"
- *Cimarron Review*: "From His Cloud in Heaven, He Comments on His Granddaughter's Post-Memorial Service Shenanigans"
- *Curbside Review*: "I Stop Lying"
- *Drash*: "Dismantling the House," "Some Mornings," "When War Comes to Lake Forest Park"
- *Elohi Gadugi*: "Dejeuner du Matin, Ce Matin"
- *Floating Bridge Review*: "Evening Song," "Jocasta Begs to be Remembered," "University of Notre Dame"
- *Literary Mama*: "Half of Infinity," "Motherhood," "Pregnant Lady Be Ready"
- *New Letters*: "Day Care"
- *The Onion River Review*: "Spring"
- *Paramour*: "Asking to Borrow a Friend's Husband"
- *Saranac Review*: "Saviors"
- *The Southampton Review*: "At Four Months I Visit Chicago," "On Seeing Blake's Illustrations"

"University of Notre Dame" was awarded honorable mention in the *Thomas Merton Poetry of the Sacred Contest*, 2003.

"The New Joke" was anthologized in *A Fierce Brightness: Twenty-Five Years of Women's Poetry,* edited by Margarita Donnelly, Beverly McFarland, Micki Reaman, and Carla Simmons Oles (Corvallis, Oregon: Calyx Books, 2002).

I am grateful to the teachers and mentors who believed in me, guided me, and pushed me intellectually and artistically: Abbe Blum, John Engman, Stuart Friebert, Barbara Helfgott Hyett, Deborah Keenan, A. J. Levine, Judy Lightfoot, Karen Mikolasy, Jim Moore, David Nash, and Jim Wichterman among so many others; to all those in classes and workshops with me who offered their care and wisdom, particularly my current readers: Pam Ingalls, Deirdre Murano, Nancy Niemczyk, nannette cotton pawlowski, Peggy Shafer, and Ellie Weiss; to those who helped so much in the preparation of this manuscript: Rebecca Moore, Susan Rich, and Mitch Reinitz; to my family for all their love and support, especially my children David Palmieri and Rose Palmieri; and, for everything, John Palmieri.

Table of Contents

Comfort

Some Mornings

Welcome to America

Don't stare Bewildered, beautiful,
Henry, Rose. *Don't cough*

Their real names thrown overboard like rags.
I wish I'd worked *Don't rub an eye*

on Ellis Island so when their bodies
Don't shuffle in ankle length overcoats

let loose the slurs and grunts of Talmudic
study, the glide of bread, *Don't breathe*

that way the deep forests, I could say,
Welcome to America *Don't stand too straight*

then trumpet back to them, their names,
write down the stones and roads,

their villages, *Don't hover* their parents'
names and their grandparents'

blessings and burden, *Don't crouch*
come into the new world.

From His Cloud in Heaven, He Comments on His Granddaughter's Post-Memorial Service Shenanigans

Afterwards, my white shirts come back
from the cleaners in plastic, preserved,
and now my granddaughter is—
big luscious tits—slipping each one
out. She's hiding in my closet,
but I can see, running her fingers down
finally, everything, every solid crease,
pulling the fabric around her,
buttoning the cuffs.
Wrong color, wrong cut, take it off!
Christ, you look as big as a house!

You know I taught drafting during the war?
I swam for U Penn. See the photo?
Now, she's cinching up my tux.
I paid for her college, my money for this lox-eating,
button-popping, cross-dressing clown.

I remember driving to the boardwalk.
The girls soft on the beach.
I told her about that. I could tell
she liked it. She's going to find
the books by the side of the bed.
She's going to try to tell the one
about the nun. She can't
fan a deck of cards either
and me a magician my whole life.

What I miss is sitting at the table by myself,
ice cream from long silver spoons.
I miss my tools: scale, tweezers, magnifying glass,
a Rotary pin in her every lapel.
She doesn't know what she's missing.

Photons

I lie in bed, gently stroke my breasts,
round as cellos. I can play them
hard like timpani, or shake them,
breath through a harmonica,

when they play the blues.

They satisfy me like abacus beads,
the rightness of math I can see.
Some mornings they are basil,
fresh and strong. Some mornings

stained glass at Chartres.

One morning soon I will
place them precisely
under the red laser line.
I will withstand photons

and electrons to save them.

Secrets

In 1969 I had secrets—cookies
I stole, dolls I buried head first
in the sand, forty thousand
Hmong carrying CIA guns.
Oh *Sarah Bernhardt* my mother
teased when I grew red
and howled. I wasn't
holding anything back—
not the North Vietnamese,
not Communism. I couldn't
cut my pot roast and carrots.
When I sipped, I spilled.
Seventeen thousand
troops, 50,000 civilians
killed. I don't remember three.
My mother told me about the dolls,
the sandbox. She showed me photos,
curly haired Debby in the high chair,
grinning through a milk mustache.
It is 1998, a Friday. Lying
on my bed in Indiana, I go looking
for needlework and learn
about my army. Fog
seeps over the fields. Someone
should have told me sooner.
Fog buries the trees, even
neon. I should have asked.
If I ventured outside, I would be
blinded in brittle snow. If I stomped,
blades of grass would crack.
Frozen mud pits sink under footprints,
the Plain of Jars under bombs.

The Hmong Hold Their History

Daughters trail their fingers through the dust.
They pick rocks from the fields of dust.
 Hunched over steel needles, they lick thread,
pull our wishes for the new year—rain, surcease
for the old and unforgiven—a thin red line
wavering and tightening through their pursed lips.

Back Then, French Fries

When she was fifteen, she would
stand outside, smoke in a white top
that tied behind her neck,

the strings so long they slithered.
This is before she knew a dick
would point up when a boy lay down.

She thought it would stick
straight out like a handle, but the first one
she saw when the boy who drawled

her name yanked down his jeans
on the Burger King bathroom floor
was flat on his belly. Then she couldn't

see anymore, just hear his rough
breath, her shoulder blades
rocking against the tiles.

When he was done, she stuffed
a wad of paper between her legs,
walked out alone, uncaught.

That was back when she sucked down
every malt she could find and ate French fries
like there would never be enough salt.

Kol Nidre

—For my high school philosophy teacher

To be swallowed by cellos
and smoke like Buber's thou—
it is not outside you, it stirs
in the depths of you—I took
that secret pleasure, scrambled

through Augustine's rubble
and squeezed by Descartes'
sharp angles. I put out my hands and felt
Nietzsche's blunt cold walls.
And Plato, I sent my cry out,
and felt it come back in my bones.

I meant to carry the gold back:

What is true and just?
I am human. I am not the only one.

It's Kol Nidre again.
I find myself thinking of you.
On this night, another chance.
Your belief in me so easily
pours into my cup. I sip it
nightly. Let it travel my veins.

Traveling Blues

Apollo, as an old man,
offers his arms. His frame's solid
like you'd expect from a god
or a man who's been dancing
his whole life, right arm in waltz hold,
palms pressing high and away.

I follow a few steps—shift, pause,
shift and then he dissolves
the space, bodies flush, hands laced.
He lifts and places on the nape
of his neck, my soft white willing hand.

He is pulsing with Bo Diddley *I'm a man,*
way past twenty-one. His thumb
caresses the edge of my thumb.
Ten white candles in small glass bowls
light their way down my spine.

Apocrypha

My lover, the mathematician, can never win a
Nobel. Legend says Nobel's wife ran off with a
geometer. From that day to this, Nobel cursed
all mathematicians like the curses of our fables,
but the modern day curse—no money or
power or fame.

I imagine the mathematician and the wife
literally running, black raincoats flapping at
their heels, boots splashing across a
cobblestone square. She giddy, a little unsteady
on the slippery stones. He holding an umbrella
and her hand. They are running not to catch a
train or to escape the dogs but for joy and
space. I never let them get to the road where
they have to wait panting for the trucks to
pass. I never worry that she has a stitch in her
side. I keep the rain slow and steady. I let them
run.

Some days I picture them running across a
park in Italy. They're still happy. It's early
morning in summer before the day tears itself
apart from heat. They have been eating fresh
peaches. Now they race to the fountain. He
slips in his leather shoes. She throws hers off
and dashes into the spray. All the old men on
iron benches watch as they chase. One snorts
and looks for her ring.

Today, I think they have stopped running. They
are in Venice. It's morning, and they are on the

verandah. The sliding glass doors stick on their runners. They sit at the remains of breakfast. He is solving theorems. She is tossing croissant to the doves. Some of it lands in the canal. Some of it floats away. I can't tell if they are happy. I can't tell if she wants to be running over bridges. I can't tell what she feels when she enters a cathedral and traces those circles on the floor, those careful mosaics of math. He is even hazier to me. What is he doing with paper and pencil? What does he see? He has never tried to explain. He puts the problem down and leans against the rail with her, the warm metal against his ribs. If he puts his arm on her shoulder, she will still be there. He can't believe she is still there.

Admitted for Observation

My uncle, the dentist, announces:
I'll care for the plants.
He waters from the fifth floor to the first,
grumbling,
dry soil, dry soil, lack of sun.

In the front hall, a rubber tree
crouches by the threadbare couch.
He grabs a branch, shakes
the leaves so hard they
strike a psychiatrist. *Who is in charge,*

my uncle bellows, *of this dead earth?*
A nurse finds a clay pot, eases
the roots out under his random orders.
He leaves his muddy prints
for the night staff to clean.

By the next day, held by the state,
he plants red-centered coleus,
the leaves the waves at Brigantine.
If he stands at the window's edge,
bricks will crumbles, azaleas bloom.

Hubris

I'm trying to learn things I need. This week
I am learning gods. Apollo answered
questions, drove his chariot daily.
I answer questions: easy ones—my zip
code, what I want for Christmas (a welcome
mat, firewood); harder ones—what I will
do for money. I can't file. I mean
I can; I have hands, I know "n" after
"m," but who will I be with paper cuts,
silent bent spine in a manila sea?

The story I tell of myself at twenty
has been cut into strips.
I know there was gelato, rain, a train
station where I screamed and cried.
I know I found Turkish Delight
abandoned beneath a bench.

I remember the first man to walk
the Uffizi with me, to see Venus
arrive from her shell; she is always
arriving with him and his long red hair,
his shy grin as we stand, touching.

Apollo stood the death of his son, death
of his lover, guilt. He cried for one day,
but back before dawn, slapping the horses
his bulging veins shoving blood to his heart.
The story he tells himself—he is what
the world needs, all lost, no fish, no fowl,
no slow opening flowers, if he gave
into grief, abandoned his job, lived true.

A Month After the Wedding

We are standing on Aurora.
Cars slug past big box stores
behind their asphalt moats, exhaust
in the air like panic. John says,
I've been making a list for our
dream house. I say, *oh, tell me.*

He lists everything:

two floors; five sinks; four windows
in the front room light
that will fade our white couch—

faded already, the cushions
that slip, the ink stain—the couch
we never think to replace; light in a hall
spreading rectangles, long warm ones
for curling up and reading instead
of picking scraps off the floor,
my scraps, he tolerates.

He lists walls for the books we carted
Boston to Minneapolis (two copies
Brothers Karamazov, a full shelf
of future worlds), back to Boston
(add laconic detectives) to South Bend
(exchange fantasy for food science)
to Seattle (add in how-to).

He talks about a house with a face
like a carved apple, shrunken
into itself, finding its own paths,
the rivulets of old age, the good bones.

I have never before been where the night sky
opens wet and smears pink, orange,
glittering purple but right now,
we are standing on Aurora.

I think *who is this man?*
I could love him.

Florence Nightingale, you were born a tree

planted in the upper crust, pruned. When you snuck
to the river view, dragged back, your mother snapped,
how could you — one of ours exposed, you'll kill me. So you
     stayed
and watched your needles yellow and drop until God
called: *cut yourself apart.*
                              You rebuilt as planks
and thwarts. From your heartwood you fashioned a keel
and a high sharp bow. Oh, you were a fierce boat.
You took Crimea with a full fleet. You
were the war's only hero. The generals chopped
you to kindling, the bits and pieces that prop
open side doors, your sawdust in the found-
ation of hospitals. One leg carved
and covered in lace for a settee. You bore weight.
A groan? A squeak? A muffled Cassandra, screaming.

The Artist Speaks to His Models

My dears you will be forever
     young as you are my glorious
dears right now. I will make you
     the mountain he ascends. You sir,
you are a man who knows
     how to kneel. Brace yourself
like love; we must see
     the muscle coil and hold. No pity
for the penitent. Bury strife
     in her skin, the hard arch of her rib.
Your head must brush
     below her breasts like a breeze
on the beaches of Nice.
     The clay glistens and turns
in my hands. I feel
     vision sliding down my palms.
I cant my head like a lover.
     I cant my head like a goddess.
May we hold this forever.

This Year's Number One Name

Say Hannah, picture a child—
button up shoes, a white frilled apron.
She's holding a pincushion,
a doll she made herself.
Her life lit by candles.
Some days we've wanted her life.

Hannah, just seventeen,
and leaning towards college, wears purple
ball gowns and wants a revolution.
Root for her.
She masks her scars
with foundation. In school

we studied Hannah.
She was the second wife, barren,
the priests thought her drunk when she prayed.
She gave her son
after craving so long. Empty,
she walked away from those stairs.

In Israel, hordes of Hannahs
in olive green, carry machine guns.
They hitchhike from the kibbutz,
sit politely in the back.
They follow orders.
They have no children to give up.

If it is the New Year

in 18th century Korea and the itinerant painter
comes to your door with wards
against evil, invite him
over the threshold. On your gate

magpies will appear, mischievous.
With strokes bold
as the mountains, you will exorcise
ghosts, show gratitude. You know

these shrine deities, the glowering
eyes under the pine, will protect
your children. You believe in the great work:
bring food to their mouths, wisdom

to their pale palms. You don't mention,
even as the tiger arches his back,
unfurls his red tongue,
if only I were at court, this would be silk.

Desire

Dejeuner du Matin, Ce Matin

Forty-four, married, two kids, I'm wandering
through Jacques Prevert like a kid kicking fall
when suddenly Kellogg Middle School,
Mr. Pierre's 7th grade French class. I'm fat.
My buckle back jeans bulge. I am afraid
of the Ayatollah Khomeni and the girl
who slammed Kiki's head in the lockers.
With smudged pencil I've filled in
the verb "to be," badly. And then I turn and I am
at a café in Paris. It's coming through my skin,
the sound of the spoon against the cup,
the sound of the rain, the sound of the chair scraping
as the man rises and leaves without a word.
Some day I will touch the back of a man's hand
at the base of the Eiffel Tower. Some day
I will sip history from snail shells.
Some day I will love beyond understanding.
I put my head in my hands and I cry.

On Seeing Blake's Illustrations

I have looked through the window then
stripped my clothes and shook my hips
in the garden. I was fourteen and ready

for the rain. My wet flesh
under the fluorescent lights of New Jersey
trying for ecstasy. Here at the Met,
Blake's craft behind glass, I am arrested
by color—yellow, red. I am trying

to conceive, have failed. The tyger
I dreaded as if I were the lamb
gazes out with a lopsided grin.
I cannot know I will bear a child,
that she will be whole,
that her heat will flood my body.

Asking to Borrow a Friend's Husband

Your husband is a map of Paris and I am
splashing through the Pompidou fountains.
He is a wildfire taking over Montana.
making the skyline hazy. He fills the air with heat.

I want your husband to glide into my dance class
in a long red shirt, swirl me
onto the floor, drunk
on fall light and the pale bewildered
faces of the students
who turn golden, who turn red, who lightly
tumble to the ground.

I want his breath
to make the curtains quiver and
flow over my skin like a ghost.

I want to slip my hands under that shirt,
to be on my knees, sink my mouth down
like the last bee finding the last bloom.

Children Die

In this festival, little children called human
sacrificial papers died there on the mountain tops.
  —Primeros Memoriales

Children die
on streets with cracked cement
and crushed dandelions. Children die swathed
in cotton dyed with indigenous
pink flowers, in fleece reconstituted
from recycled plastic bottles.
Children die under tree limbs,
beside bombed out burnt carburetor parts, in
    the desert
where the birds land. Children stop breathing.
Children die under fluorescent lights,
in the pith of intellectual rigor. Children die
in the womb. They abandon us.
Children die of crushed bones,
broken genes. Children drown.
Children fall from high places. They make
Rorschach patterns we fail. Children leave
with the ghosts who live underground.
Children die of snake bite,
rock slide, bear hide, dolphin ride.
Children die of love. Dried up
rivers of children.

Up the mountain the Aztecs carried
their toddlers, petulant and kicking,
their nursing infants tied to their breasts.
I feel my child's warm skin in my hands,
the soft spot on her cranium.
I lay her body across my heart beat
and she sleeps, her small fist in my throat—
my sweet monkey, my bunny, my lamb.

Still Life

I am looking for death.

It is a game we play, Van Dyck and I,
among hard rinds,
the apple peel that slithers
off the white lace cloth, pulsing grapes
the last moment before

they burst. Van Dyck has found
a gilded shell to set
in a long metal stem. One could
sip wine from its blue body.

I want it.

I want life to my lips.
I want to eat at this banquet even
when death hovers. I could serve
in a white lace neckpiece.
I could crack nuts, rest my teeth
against the fragile rim

and not bite down, just feel
the cool scrape
against my tongue. I've never
walked a frozen pond, felt it start
to thaw. (I kissed a boy,
more than one.)

Rumpelstiltskin hunches in the corner,
busy with straw. I never called out
for that kind of help even when I found

a bird's broken body in the basement well,
saw, on a friend, skin soft and paled as butter.
Van Dyck holds a dinner knife
to my neck. I feel its cool blunt edge.

I call it pearls.

Half of Infinity

Once I saw two
ropes turning.

I couldn't see the ocean
ends. I watched

them slowly come back
to themselves. A friend

swam with dolphins
at five months. A pup

close to her belly. The guide
said, *He hears the second*

heartbeat; he doesn't understand
how this can be. Nor me. Nor me.

Pregnant Lady, Be Ready

At the drugstore,
strangers will stare.

They'll hoot and holler
about ice cream for two,

insist on carting
your bag. Later

they will wonder if you can
do your job. They will know

you've had sex. They'll picture
you having sex, your clothes off.

You can't remember if you just shoved
your gown aside. You remember how

the wind shook the windows.
They will say your life will never be

the same; you'll never sleep again. And then
they'll tell you of the pancakes that they make.

Strangers will lay hands on you.
They'll point out eye sockets

and elbows, show you
shadows. Like a gypsy

in one tale, or fairies
from another,

they will come
after your fate.

At Four Months Pregnant, I Visit Chicago

1. The art museum

Renoir's laundress, puts
her basket down, hands on her hips,
a slightly rounded belly.
Maybe she has a secret,
I have a secret!

2. The natural history museum

I have waited in line for an hour.
The history of chocolate is the history of slaves.
Children crowd in front.
I step around their screams and vomit.
In the jade room, intricate, quiet,
a baby doll in white flannel lies crumpled
beside the glass case.

3. The night club

Bathed in pink neon and the futile
gyrations of the children, yes they are just
children, and they don't
see me, never mind
my spandex. I drink tonic,
bargain with smoke.

4. In line at the windowless McDonald's

cattle car railings, no natural light,
the desperate hope that they will still have
fish filet like I used to get on Sundays
like I used to get at the Philly Street Station
like I used to get driving Minneapolis to Seattle
listening to Sherlock Holmes
and Lolita, I find a place.

5. Walking Wabash

Brancusi's Sleeping Muse has
no body, closed stylized eyes.
I have a complete body, every finger, every
limb.
I move like a gracious mountain.
I could. I will be a lahar, carving the plain.
My eyes wide open even in the wind.

Saviors

I was hoping for Hercules, but he's just too dumb.
Sure he's strong, frankly none stronger. If I needed

a truck hauled by hand through a tsunami, he'd be
my man. But when he gets hot, he cocks

his arrow at the sun. He yells and believes
the waves will still. I see him in the lifeguard chair.

I might be a teenybopper clustered at the base.
I could bleach and pluck and hope a string

bikini makes me one of the crowd. The one picked.
I wanted to be a savior, but Angela, my student

whose high heels travel through gravel and mud,
cannot learn the paragraph. I'm not talking

concept here, like when a new idea begins;
I'm talking a push on the tab key,

an index finger exerting a little pressure. Every time
she doesn't hit it (and she doesn't ever) I fail.

I failed trolling after Hercules, but I met Atlas
up to his neck in darkness, up to his brows in clouds.

Night and Day don't stop to bring him water.
Once he had a chance to save himself. But along came

Hercules, *Here, buddy, could you hold this? I'll be right back.*
I've been tricked into taking back a video, paying

a bus fare. I wonder if that's happened to Angela?
She's so steady, will hold one idea—her right to think

spiritually which means, as far as I can tell, without
logic or coherency, with only the sounds

of scripture and not their sense—in her tight-fisted brain
until the rest of us crack and turn to dust. Even Atlas

might stumble: she'll beat her breast, preach that word.
The mole between my breasts has turned darker I think.

It's the one that marks the boundary: you look nice
tonight do you have to dress like that. I've loved it

all my life. Angela would condemn my carnal mind.
Atlas too burdened to look. I could stop reading it

like Braille, my fingers over the oval. I could see
a doctor. It's probably nothing, my imagination.

I need to pick up the phone, press a few keys.
Sorry, so terribly sorry, that would be Hercules.

Even in the Rain

It's raining. A real bitch of a rain, a cats falling
on top of, kicking the dogs to the curb rain.
You couldn't even claim anything
about devils grabbing lightning bolts
like wish bones, breaking them in half.
There aren't any—devils, bolts.
Just closed shutters. Dark takes a broom
to the street and sweeps up the currents of
wherever you need to go.

Is the world washing away like cinnamon
from the foam of cocoa? Yes, you almost
    remember
the taste, almost remember the place
you found and you do have a favorite
place in Nice where they sell candied almonds,
drenched and drowned in rain.

If you could find the way, you could have
a sweeping talk with the devil. He'd gut you,
of course, or poison your mind
with nuclear plants, the slow drip
into the sands. Just pretend
those sands aren't stained.

Cherries in the thick brown bowl
taste of patience.
Put them at the center of the discussion.
They don't doubt. They wouldn't dream
of being agnostic. They know
the bell rings even in the rain.

You need the bucket with the broken
white handle, the shovels and when they break,
you need your hands, tightly held,
grimy, dripping wet, straining in the rain.

Motherhood

My parents want grandkids.
They've been asking,
When are you going to give us
grandkids?

They've saved wooden blocks
in a barrel. They long to hold
the smooth edges again, make
a train track to Uzbekistan,

a tower to the moon. Pete Seeger's
cued up, the actual record,
all around the kitchen cockadoodle
doodle do.

I picture myself with a son—
six years old in plastic boots.
Let's make them yellow.
He has cinnamon sugar glazing his skin.

He takes my hand in an April rain.
I stamp. He stamps twice.
We giggle down the sidewalk, swing
our arms and sing nonstop.

He wades into cattails and skunk cabbage.
Burrowing, his blue windbreaker barely
crowns the fallow ground.
I don't call. I don't wait. I walk away.

When War Comes to Lake Forest Park

We'll buy in bulk: drums of chili, twenty-four
freeze-dried paper cups of chive potatoes.
We'll cull our books. A friend survived Iran's
revolution hiding hers with the underground.
She couldn't bear to burn Jane Eyre, Macbeth.
Books burned in Sarajevo. Two or three
to boil water. Perhaps, we could start
with the workbooks for words we never learned,
add the atlas. We'll need to make our own
light. Current will cut out
like every winter when wind
takes down the pines. This time
bombs will take down the pines.
Bombs will take us to the edge of the lake.
Children, off their bikes, will be in bulk.
They'll keep up the bonfire, huddle in
to drain the last of the raspberry Kool-aid.

The New Joke

I'm drawing a picture of a chicken.
I put black magic marker to scratch paper and
    voila, a chicken.
Then I phone my sister.
I tell her, *In front of me is a picture of a chicken.*
She says, *I see it.*
I say, *I am going to point to the parts of the chicken*
and you are going to name them, but you must
    never say
this part here.
Which part? she says.
This part which flaps ineffectually. This part more
    bone
than meat that Mom would crack and chew for the
    marrow.
She says, *Oh that part.*
Instead, I want you to name this part.
The breast, she says. *Right,* though
I have pointed at nothing.
This? the tail. This? the beak.
Now put your left pinkie to your lips, curl your
    fingers in
to your cheek and jaw, and put your thumb to your
    ear.
She says *I've done it.* I believe her.
I want you to say that word three times slowly.
Wing. Wing. Wing.
Hello? Who is it?
She falls off the couch.
She is laughing so hard. *Oh God, I have to pee.*
    We both

race to the toilet the portable phones gasping
   and hooting between.
I say *Hello? Hello?*
We are both rolling on the tile floor tears
   screaming.
When we pause for breath she says, *Mom's
   tests came back you know.*
I know I say to my sister curled around the
   toilet base, sobbing.

I Stop Lying

This is the day after
the day I broke the promise.

This is the day after a breakwall
of regret between me and sleep heavy so

I couldn't hear its waves just my own
head pounding. The day I couldn't

eat a corner of dry toast.
My hand wouldn't lift.

My lips wouldn't open.
This is the day I have told him.

In his arms I told him.
This is the day he cries.

This is the day I don't break
an etched plate from Paris, no

invisible slivers across the floor,
the table square on the red faded rug.

This is the day years before the alarm,
so loud our bones ache. Then we move—

he downstairs. I go to find him.
He is standing in water the color of steel.

He looks stunned, drained of hope.
I take his hand. I pull.

Spring

A morning squall outside my window.
The crow hunts fledglings, shakes
the new blossomed tree like tattered lace.
When a song bird falls, the cat takes wing.

Day Care

The first day

Rose is fourteen months. That's over a year. Some kids start at six weeks. She lies on her mat crying. We can hear it through the door. We look in at her body under the frog blanket, the exact one we use in her crib. The woman says we will disturb the kids. When Rose falls into my arms, her crying stops.

I carry her half a mile home, past the bread company outlet, past dogs, their leashes draped around lampposts, past the flower shop, the barber, the antiques store, the corner diner. The whole way she doesn't cry.

At a month

Rose eats. For two weeks she wouldn't. Spare clothes, all labeled, hard-soled shoes as required. Fell down the cement steps twice, stays sitting at circle time.

Circle time

Some days I stay for circle time. I am trying to learn everything—story, song, story. Elongate the vowels. Do you know what color this is? I sing. I clap. I sit crisscross applesauce. I wait for my name to be called.

The day I sit on the floor

Back against the wall, lift my shirt, lift my bra,
nurse my baby, my baby girl.

In the fall leaves

We have closed the door to unit one, gone up
the basement steps, gone past the fenced-in
woodchips. Three blocks away Rose stops. She
has something to say. Her body quivers—"bell,
loud, bell, no coat, outside."

"Oh! Was there a fire drill? Was there a big bell,
and you went outside without your coat on?
Was it loud? Was it exciting?" I have
understood her exactly. We both jump up and
down. We both grin. She grabs my hands and
we swing.

The day it hails

The children cannot see the ghosts drumming
at the window. I want to show Rose, but I am
afraid it won't be fair. I want to be fair to all
children, to hold them in my arms, to be the
mother that has come early, the magic one.
Rose lets the teacher lift her. *Erika,* she says,
Erika, Erika, Erika all the slick and dark way
home.

Erika

She's having a cigarette on the back steps, crying. Her ex won't pay the child support. He can't. He won't. Just one hundred a month. I think about slipping it into the teacher pouch next to the grown-ups' bathroom, the one I sneak into when I'm desperate. I think about putting together a basket of fruit or baking banana bread. I haven't baked since Rose was born. She thought they might be getting back together. She has to go to the food bank. She has to go back to class.

Comfort

University of Notre Dame

Jesus is everywhere here,
usually, dying or dead.

When he was still a Jew like me,
Jesus would
go where women go, to the well.
Do the forbidden—talk
to women, even Samaritans.

He would know
women's secrets before they spoke them.
He would not judge.

That is the Jesus
I finally find. Outdoors,
cast in bronze, one hip
balanced on the lip of the well
a living hand lifted.

What would they do, the Christians, if I sat
      next to Jesus?
What would they do if I
put my arms around
the warm rusted metal of his back?

Oh I am so lonely here.
Jesus, rabbi,
before you become a martyr,
comfort me.

The Screening

First I am late,
        then wrong
                building, wrong floor,
                        then
I am really late
        and keep racketing
                down long barren
                        corridors
like in the dream
        where I cannot find
                Alice's world.
                        I look for
WOMEN
        MATERNAL INFANT
                and find
                        bassinets
right there,
        the excruciatingly
                small hands
                        swathed.
I collapse
        and bawl.
                I have watched
                        children with Down's,
the skinny girl
        at the pool
                playing catch.
                        The boy
under the concrete bridge
        who shouted
                to the echoes.
                        I would never

walk up to the ark
        on my own,
                pull the curtain,
                        touch
the blue and white
        embroidered flowers,
                the Torah cover,
                        the Torah.
The bored tech
        waves a wand
                over my belly
                    and
Niobe bragged
        about her children,
                so they were all
                        slain
by the gods.
        When I imagine
                the fetus I carry
                    heartbeat,
limb buds, my child,
        I see her whole,
                hugging me
                    like the girl
at the party,
        Tay Sachs, trisomy 18,
                Down's,
                  spina bifida,
cystic fibrosis,
        didn't even know me,
                just held her arms
                    open.

Under a Sliver of Moon

In the 4 a.m. dim dark your in-drawn
breath I am turning before I have left
sleep I am lifting my body my breast
to your body straining panting toward
the scent of one long hard nipple wet
your tongue pulls down I am under

The Last Few Days Before Christmas

At the big box store every parking space full,
the cart full of rain, the store full of souls
anxious to find just a gallon of milk
to make it through morning, David, almost a
    year,
looks at the ceiling, as far away as faith—
all white, light after light.

I know that children ask us to see is a cliché.
But this is my baby.
For five fallow days, he has cried.
So if he stops in Fred Meyer, the cereal aisle,
if he tips his head back, glows with his grin,
if his whole body says, *can I get an amen?* I say
    amen, amen.

Happiness Survey

I am taking a happiness survey.
Three times a day I am asked:
Am I happy?
I say, happy, mostly happy.
I choose traffic,
dishes, to hug my girl
though she stomps away.

I'm on a swing that lifts
me into the air though
it's not the slab
of wood painted spring
sun on crocus red
that keeps me from falling to the ground,
but the repulsion of vibrant electrons.

Feel them now
singing a hallelujah chorus
in the cathedral of matter.
Know them as a matter
of faith. Oh the bonds,

gravity broken and rejoined,
thrills me as I swing through.

I Ask Demeter to Waltz

I've been to dances without any friends.
know what it's like, to sit on the side.
I've spent the dance on the edge of my chair,
and I have not been asked.

Yes, I am a woman, but I am not
a thief. See me as your daughter
but not as naïve, not apple cheeked,
blossoms don't grow from these hands.

Goddess pretending to be an old woman,
brows penciled in, powder pale skin,
I stand before you my palm facing up.
Don't cut your eyes and decline.

I have learned to lead, so I
can bite off time. Pomegranate seeds
sections of loss, for the space of a song,
let my arms form a frame for sorrow.

Dismantling the House

We take the Alaskan, the African, the Balinese masks.
The ornate screws that hold up the screen.
We take door handles. Lace parasols tear.

We take the peaceful wooden beads,
the peaceful wooden fish. We take
the front hall bathroom papered with trees.

We take our last time at the Seven Seas diner,
limp beans, pork chops
that make me keen and gnaw.

We take the last time at the bank where every teller
knows my grandfather's name, where the ladies check
if I've gained weight.

We take the shopper's parking lot,
the girl I watched buy
velvet jodhpurs for her Bat Mitzvah.

We take Broadway plays. Chock full o'Nuts
before opera. We take the proper scarf,
the stiff wool hat that scratched.

From the boys' bathroom, we take the cracked
blue toilet seat cover.
The way the door had to be slammed three times
before it would latch.

We take screams.
We take the whole Jewish world.

What I Would Take With Me

—For Ingie now 100 living in Anderson House

The coffee maker—that's first.
The toaster oven for tuna melt.

I've been looking at places, you know,
with the small small cupboards and the small
small rooms. Where would you put this?
Where would you put that?

I have to take the Toby jug because
during the war my brother
with the 101st Airborne sent it
wrapped in parachute silk.

I'm not taking my sterling.

I would take my little Norway spoons.
They show the Maltese cross.
When the King of Norway
went down to conquer everyone,
he got Christianized instead.

My rolling pin, handcarved for making Lefze.
(If you're Norwegian you know.)

I've been giving cups away.

I would have to have room
for a table with a lace cloth.
A lace tablecloth is just part of life.

At the Edge

Michelle, who shares every detail of the day,
scared stiff but benign, three times; Kathleen
who teases—same; Rosemary who doesn't
always trust me—surgery in late January; Mom
—lumpectomy, the drain, six weeks radiation
driving herself daily, lymph nodes cut,
circulation cut, movement curtailed; for
Mordena, who nursed, add chemo; Rebecca, a
silver knife—more chemo, lost hair, bone deep
fatigue; Ingie next door, Sue in Ohio, the
librarian with the red and white scarf—
mastectomy, radiation, chemo; Linda (Ingie's
daughter)—legs wouldn't lift;

on lucky days, on days when a woman is
blessed with no children to gather and
disburse, no geese to lure across the hard
brown dirt, no wash to lift and wring and beat,
no men to appease, she can lie by the side of a
stream, her blouse loosened so the sun scoops
under her breasts; she can bring her body
down by a quiet river; she can leave the earth;

when I leave the earth, a cat yowls; I walk up
to the woman at the library and say, *I saw you
in my dream, standing behind this desk*; she clasps
my hands between hers, large and dry; she
invites me to touch her breast, the one that's
left; I let my hand be lifted; her nipple talks to
my thumb, continents swirl and melt; one of us
is Atlas.

Jocasta Begs to be Remembered

I did not ask that he be an athlete
or miner or blessed by the gods, but I heard
boys who were touched by their mothers
became the best lovers, so I vowed
to touch my son.

I let him crawl in my lap when I needed
to eat. I moved my spoon
around his flailing body.
I let him crawl in my bed when I needed
to sleep and plastered
his jutting ribs to my bladder,
and I didn't cry, oh let me be!
I let him be.

I kissed him.
You think I won't admit to that?
I kissed his toes, his nose,
his knees, the soft down of his neck,
the underside of his thighs.
I kissed his elbows while he held
my nipple in his mouth.

He kissed me
on the cheek, on the nose,
on the chin, on the elbow.
He leapt into my arms to kiss me.

There he is, almost five,
in his green and white shirt,
holding hands with the girl
with pony tails. He drapes his arm
over her shoulders. He kisses her cheek.

Where did he learn to dangle
his fingers down, so she will
reach up and touch them?
She touches them.

Five Forever

Every day, my son will shock me
saying please when he stops me

talking. He wants to hear
how the Swallows and Amazons

shoot arrows, sail boats, fight for the island.
With his red racer toothbrush, he will

brush his bare butt (*You said butt!*
You said butt!) and cry when I pry it away.

He will eat only cheddar on rice,
golden raisins, eat them with his fingers

and talk through each bite. He will hug
his sister knock over hard, launch

to my arms full body on. He will refuse
to put on his coat with the broken zipper

even when it's cold, even when it's
pouring rain. He will know

without counting what happens
when one banana is taken away.

All day he will say, *Avast there*
Peggy you goat! and laugh and laugh.

My Daughter and I Discuss Nuclear Bombs over Breakfast

My hand grows old in this ring, God willing.
Skin splatters and shrinks, splotches to
    camouflage,
but diamonds will catch the sun, distilling
fusion, flash blue, flash green, a sung collage
to the star at the center. Diamonds recruit
librettos even as my breath grows still.
If I'm blessed, a grandchild alive, astute
will warm my lap. She'll turn my wrist and fill
her palms, slight soft, with aleatoric light.
I see us on a long green lawn, the hum
of August, me and my grandma, our right
clasped hands. Surely, there must have been a
    diamond
but all I see—honeysuckle, the bees,
a sway of the hammock between the trees.

To the Med Students About to Butcher my Body

I forgive you.
I forgive the way the scalpel
trembles ever so slightly
or the way it doesn't.

I forgive you for seeing
stretch lines on my thighs, marbling fat
my flesh unshaven,
the way my smallest toes curl
to uselessness.

While living, Christopher Hitchens
asked to crack open his chest and know
if the rash on his skin also scoured
inside. I forgive you
for knowing.

I forgive you for not lifting my limp hand,
feeling the callouses at the base
of my left fourth finger, right third,
and knowing, as Sherlock Holmes
would have known in an instant, that I waited
fourteen years to marry.

I forgive you for not knowing that three years later
I sat on a bench in Barcelona while Gaudi
stretched me to new shapes, that I savored
cheese in oil. I forgive you for not feeling
the weight of my baby sleeping
as I eat paella in the sun.

Evening Song

When my daughter, straight from her bath,
brings her body to mine
and she has no breasts and she has only
the slightest dip in the straight line that is her
still damp with the equinox,
when she molds her body to mine,
her head under my head, her long rib cage
against my deep breasts, our heartbeats
a processional, then I know
what is in the hands Rodin
sculpted and called Cathedral.

Deborah Bacharach's poems have been published in journals nationally and internationally, including *The Antigonish Review, Arts & Letters, Calyx, Cimarron Review, New Letters* and *Poet Lore*. She studied at Swarthmore College and the University of Minnesota. She is a college writing instructor, editor, and tutor. She lives in Seattle with her family.

CPSIA information can be obtained
at www.ICGtesting.com
Printed in the USA
FSOW02n1259100415
6298FS